The Stains of Burden and Dumb Luck

FIRST EDITION, 2017

Stains of Burden and Dumb Luck
© 2017 by Carolyn Dunn

ISBN 978-0-9972517-7-7

Except for fair use in reviews and/or scholarly considerations, no part of this book may be reproduced, performed, recorded, or otherwise transmitted without the written consent of the author and the permission of the publisher.

Cover Art
The Stains of Burden © 2017 by Eric Ruiz (Karuk)

Author Photo
© 2017 Tierney Shawnee

Mongrel Empire Press
Norman, OK

Online catalogue: www.mongrelempire.org

This publisher is a proud member of

COUNCIL OF LITERARY MAGAZINES & PRESSES
www.clmp.org

The Stains of Burden and Dumb Luck

Carolyn Dunn

2017

Contents

Prologue
    Bloodline   1

I. Some Other World
    Storyteller   5
    In Some Other World   7
    Deer Blood   9
    Gravity   10
    Indian Time   11
    Singing the Sky   13
    World Renewal   15
    Sleeping Giant   16
    Redbird   18

II. Stained
    Backyard Astronomy   21
    Anniversary   23
    Stay   24
    Spoils   26
    Grace   27
    Quartet   28
    Words   30
    Nocturne   34
    The Daughter of the Sun   35

III. Baskets Filled With Burdens
    The Other Daughter of the Sun   39
    Afterglow   42
    I Must Keep Myself   44
    The Rapture   46
    Chaconne   47
    Inheriting Her Brother's Horse   49
    Kama'aina   51
    Twilight   52
    Cardinal Direction   53

IV. The Knot At The End Of The World
    The Water Monster   59
    I Met an Old Woman   60
    Hanalei   62
    The Knot at the End of the World   63
    Global Positioning System   65

Epilogue
    How we end(ed)   69

Prologue

The Real People, once so great and formidable, will be compelled to seek refuge in some distant wilderness… We will hold our land.

~Ada-gal'kala (Attakullakulla) 1775

Bloodline

A place doesn't need to be idealized to still claim the comfort associated with being called home. To be welcomed home with open arms is to match the night's shimmering of stars and feel at one, at peace with oneself and one's place among those stars. Here, at the junction of land and stars and trees and fog and ocean and somewhere else, that trail has grown cold.

A distant fire burns at the rim of the hollow of the eyes of the desperate ones. They listen to the source of the mystery, but answer in a voice that cannot be silenced.

It is the power in the voice of the soul that has been recovered, restored to beauty from the ghost world. The songs that keep hold of the digest of desperation entrenched in the songs of a dispossessed people is part of that world that must be cut away in order to survive.

That which is cut cannot be defined by its other half, its missing piece, its soul wound. The deepest part of night is that piece which cannot be named. Patterns exist in a person's life that were woven long before their first breath is drawn.

Woven in the bone and blood of the Ancestors, it is now a tapestry concerted with keeping of stories, vocalized in song, in whispers, in secret, from stages and from graveyards and birthing rooms around the long pathway of this world to where the next world awaits.

The patterns weave the sky in the tear of a glittering body, a curved leg of the grandmother. In the sky, she rises over misted reflections of rain, of clouds called by jimsonweed, wild alata, and sage. We will remember to look west, and the land where the sun makes her return, we follow out of desire, out of necessity, out of fear. For warmth and blessing and the calling home of our spirits to the place we shall all be reunited with once again.

Crawling out of the earth, reborn into the balance of love and death by the ladder of mud, stone and clouds, our gazes hold with the great mother in the sky, her love mending the torn centered edge, bearing the stars home on the back of her shell, given freely when the time comes for us to be reborn.

I. Some Other World

We came pouring out of the backbone of this continent like ants.

~Louis Little Coon Oliver

Storyteller
from the play Yellow Bird

(The Storyteller finishes singing, addresses the People.)

I would like to tell you all a story. Now, visitors, come here. This story concerns you as well.

(Boogers slowly begin to sit as the Storyteller begins.)

There was this woman, of the Bird Clan, who went to draw water off the Oconoluftee. This woman, now she was unmarried, she went to the water to gather it for her family. It was beautiful there, at the river. It was the time where leaves turn red, fall to the ground, hide under the blanket of snow, and renew the earth, make ready for corn. The water rushed by, fish jumped, and it was very peaceful. Beautiful. The land was alive. It was so beautiful the woman fell asleep. In her dream she saw a man come from the river, sliding wet upon the shore, shaking water off his long black hair.

(The People, including Boogers, react to the story in *oohs* and *ahhs*.)

His arms were decorated in silver bands, his eyes darkest, deepest black of the river's center in the starlight. He stood above her, blocking out trees and moon and night sky. Water ran from his body sparkling in darkness. He was really good to look at.

When the woman woke from her dream, she returned home and soon she bore a child. Her relatives were pretty offended by this, and when the child opened his eyes he had the otherworldly dark eyes of the Water Panther. Now her relatives, like I said, were pretty ashamed by this whole spectacle, so they made plans to get rid of the child.

The woman would have none of this. She went down to the river where the Water Panther lived and said to the Water Panther, "my relatives want to kill my child. I need you to help me, so they won't kill him."

The Water Panther told the woman, "tell your relatives to move their settlements closer to the river, where there is better land for farming corn. This way, they will leave you and your son alone." So the woman told them this, and her relatives moved down to the river. The Water Panther, seeing this, made the rivers rise, washing out the people's settlement.

(The Storyteller gestures with his lips for the people to look in the distance)

If you look, you can just sometimes see the top of the old ceremonial lodge in Bird Town, where the timbers didn't get washed out by the flood. When we see those timbers we remember those old times.

After the flood the Water Panther took the woman to live with him below the water.

Now, there were some people still alive after the flood and they came together to say "We need to find a new place to live, a new ground with which to bless, and be blessed by our Corn Mothers." So they looked around and found the place where the earth was red and made their towns there. Their bird town. There was water near them and sometimes when they were having dances they could hear the sound of a very faraway drum and hear voices of the people who had drowned, singing and having a good time. On the place in the old Bird Town where the people went to the water, there were whirlpools.. They were very cautious about water after that. Sometimes they could see the places where the water came together, the whirlpool, which likes to suck people underwater and cause their death by drowning. The Underwater Woman misses her relatives so much that anyone passing over the whirlpool gets caught into it. Even the birds and insects who fly over these whirlpools get caught in it and drown, except for the small brown bird with the yellow breast, the Chesquatalawny, whom the Water Panther's wife has a fondness for. I don't know why this woman likes that yellow bird so much. Maybe he reminds her of her brothers or uncles. He likes to play tricks on her maybe, telling her how beautiful she is by his song. "Swhee shwee."(The Storyteller sings a little.)

The yellow bird is a tough one, is close to the land, and that's why the Water Panther's wife likes him. She finds him beautiful. He reminds her of the beautiful river and what life was like before she went below to her husband. Before her relatives tried to kill her child. Before they left her behind.

In Some Other World

In some other world
stars shine bright
upon wounds of our
ancestors, stored in gates
leading from one place
to the next.
Songs that herald
passage of time by birth
still sung as we
enter into this world,
dreaming.
Distant reaches
of song storied
in memory
of my mother's birth
is history
recorded time
upon shells in
red, deep sunset,
and carried at
the hip as a gesture
of remembrance.

In some other world,
I speak words
of my grandmothers, their
frozen tongues speaking out of turn,
I gaze out from
behind her
eyes, singing her
world back into existence.
My mother's words
pass through my lips, echoing
across flat plains
and oceans of stars
beckons us home
with songs that bring corn.

In some other world,
the first shoot of silk
reaches toward the space
from where we all came.
Like us, they look to sky, wishing to
call back the ones who left.
Like them, a silk tuft of gold
calls the rain cloud.

This sea is strong,
grounds me here,
in space of breath, in faceted turn
of a song, my face turned to sky.
My grandmother's voice,
passing my lips
escapes the veil
of some other world.

Deer Blood

Dying
her last breath
formed a Creek Chorus

which placed
the blame squarely
on shoulders
of the hand

that fed her.

Gravity

I.
Wistful
I make my way
to shore,
confident
that sorrow
will find
me standing.

II.
Solitude.
Life on a
mountain of clear,
clean snow.

I find myself
with thoughts
of a thousand
year old red star
singing.

III.
In the house
of red light
your whispers
fade into
blue
night
air.

My house is
full
of red
light.

Indian Time

In darkness
of stars
time unfurls
we
watch light dance
upon water.

In deepening reflection,
watching unraveling
green leaf and
blowing breeze
we see
the time begun
again.

Sheltering
uncoiling reach of
what must be and what breathes
we are once again
taken by force
into revelation
of starlight.
Can we possess
what is needed
to remander the last world
before this one?

A songline appears
at center of
a portioned time.
That-Which-Moves
moves
and breathe that
signals coming
of dawn
breaches clouds.
One row folds
in upon itself
creating another, another:

each the same
as the last.
Light from bright
darkness from shadow
each sparkle
remembrance
of what is past,
what is now,
what will be.

Impenetrable
this breath
that compels
us closer towards
pure light.

Singing the Sky

In every shell, leaf, unfurling
bud of daylight, every
bleeding blossom,
there is anticipation
when water falls
from sky.
The man in the mountain
sleeps through the memory
of waking,
mourns the hearts
stolen from
beneath his wings.

This small deity,
this lost dewdrop
 has come
to know
how to make
things like rain
stay in the sky.
Flowers, plants,
trees shudder
for a knowing
that never fully comes.
Sleeping one
keeps the blessing
rain of myth and memory
to himself, entering
only into his own
dreams,
the sum of water
and earth
sluicing down
the sum of parts.

We who love this place
dream our own terror,
our own lament,
our own fall from highest sky.

This too is
our story.
Yet we claim
love rooted here
instead of fear.
That difference
between us.
Nahullo. Oka.
We cannot claim
what is not ours.
Still these songs,
Of leaf, sky, blossom,
blood from cut
glass of sand shards
color of her hair.
We know these songs,
mark the sum,
claim none as our own.

Looking to Sleeping Giant,
man made of mountain, of spring
of rain shuddering into broken earth,
dreaming he becomes
another dream of his dreaming,
Sing for rain,
ask, you said, for
his children live
inside. We are
visitors in a holy place,
named through birthright
we sing the rain home.

World Renewal

Drifting on blue sail
of shell, rock, sleet,
ever facing daunting tide.

Passing stones
between the teeth of
passing stones,
we rise, we rise.
Depths of sadness and grace falling away.
I rescind what
magic leaves on breath
taste of bitterness and grief.

I accept a
new rough song
escaping from my lips
torn by teeth and regret.
We breathe life
into dying songs.

Sleeping Giant

Rocks rise out
of wooden stake
driven through the
heart
of a dispossessed people.
When he lay down
and slept
sun was high
overhead, blistering
in her cruelty —
to those who do
not know lash
of her tongue.
Sleeping Giant
laying upon the
Canopy offers kindness
of shade and his love for us —
Though we do
nothing to
Earn his trust.
Simple acts of kindness,
a space of wind, a drop
of a heart, was
enough to turn the people
to one another.
It was their laughter
lulling him
their jokes inspirited moments —
Their shared kisses and
caresses of supplication —
Form his sacrifice.
All this that first garnered attention of those who
believe their own press.

Waking his name,
carries away power
Of faceless mountain.
Stolen like our prayers
spoken now in tongue

of our betrayer.
Our love
mere ghosts
of praise
for the Sleeping Giant. .
His name is given in law only now —
the passing of title and stolen hearts, of
minds and wounds that can't heal.

Sleeping Giant's eyes are open.
He will fully wake,
to speak his trampled name.
Rising,
Sleeping Giant will
sleep no more.

Redbird

In mist
of rain and
dappled leaves
Shining in air,
presence of deepening
sorrow and mourning lingers.

In this air,
upon this breath
the dream of flying
on sunlit oars
remains at water's edge,
those who seek their solace
in her soul.

Coming to the edge
they see above the
waterline, two steps ahead
of time and space
between meaning
and morning, tear
stained voices
filled with longing
decorate the mist
with remembrance.
they raise
their cries to heaven,
asking for a gathering
of stars and rain to be
the holding of her
breath.

II. Stained

But the Bayou St. John did not answer. It merely gathered into its silent bosom another broken-hearted romance, and flowed dispassionately on its way.

~ Alice Dunbar Nelson

Backyard Astronomy

Light rises
prepares for
high noon.
Here, it is called
the sun at her highest
point in sky,
brightest moment
of a day's life.
It was here
the sun
waited to return home,
for her daughter awaited her.
Still, something else waited.
Copperhead,
steel eyes gleaming.
Diamond-backed,
compass rose trail points to the setting
of the daylight's only star.

From the passing
of light it took
the Sun to
journey home.
Redbird was gone.
her soul a thrush and thrall
her eyes no
longer on the sky

It was an easy death.
Redbird moved
across the world
to the Ghost Country,
played for shine,
for luck,
for love,
for grace.
She could
no longer see
the sky

that traced
her ascendance
back to where
her heart began.

Stars,
so many stars,
and longing
so far away,
A tiny pinpoint
light of brightest
rarity
rushing from the dark
blanket of night sky,
which one,
she sighs,
which point
each calling her,
skwee, skwee,
is home?

Anniversary

Last year
the rains
washed
the hurt
clean.
Now
I stand
in a sorrow's desert,
dry mouthed,
alone.

Evening.
Days pass away,
stars have
grown cold
your heart
a thousand shards
of red ice
piercing veil
of my skin.

Stay

Stay,
my funny valentine.
in midst
of this chaos
is bliss,
me and you,
him and her
and her and she
and he and
she and you
from us two.
Who knew
in twinkle
of ancestral eye,
all those years
ago,
that we would end up
at the dawn of the world,
breathing an
ocean of stars
and sound
of water returning
to this land of
falling stars
and fallen angels,
Small spaces
in midst
of this newborn
and urban
sprawling of arms,
fingers,
galaxies,
patterns of stars and rain
in dirt trails and washways emptied?

At mouth
of a forgotten river,
an empty and stolen grave,
fingers reaching

for what can
never
achieve,
you and me
and he and she
and she and they
became us
against darkest
night,
reborn in earth
and stars
they breathe songs,
stolen from tongues
cut from
brick and mortar,
brought back by love
of those
who came before
and prayers
of the ancestors
who wove the pattern,
that winds us in
a story of rivers --
forgotten and remembered,
forged and forsaken,
in the eyes
of our children,
hurling back words
cut from mouths
watered and fed
by the very rain
that wanted us
dead.

Spoils

Coffee
and starlight
remind me
of your touch.
A feather
falling from a
sky lit shower
of long dead stars
and breath
from the natal charts
of ancient astronomers.
two signs,
combatant
and watchful,
meet on shore.
Lightning strikes,
meeting again and again
firelight shadows
fall from lips
of those doomed to
repeat the curse
of prophets and seers,
Those who take to
sky
for signs.
She moves among the fallen,
the days' toll
ravaged again
for souls
of men.

Cream or sugar,
you said in that voice
laced with both;
Spoils, I said,
greedy for the tribute
due me.

Grace
for Michael

"I seen the spirits
dance on that one,"
he said, when the song was finished.
"They stood at the
water and waved."
Then you waved back.

"It's the power of
that song," I said, "that line
connecting me to you and
this home country
to my heart.
Now my home is in
your heart. That's
The power of this song,
"That's the power of these Ancestors,"
I say, "for we are a dispossessed
Hatak Okla, in the shadows of our
colonized civilized propagandized
broken and bleeding
hearts."

We sat in silence a moment,
watching the sky dance
upon the break
of shore, lashing the
world with wind,
water and light,
dispossessed spirits
with the grace of motion
to never, ever
cease the wandering,
breath into being, soul
into survivance,
from your heart to mine,
and back again.

Quartet

I.
Midwinter.
World spins
on a foreign shore.
We form alliances
leaving behind
bones of
our sorrow
in balls of glass
shattered
and worn
on sand.

II.
Moon
whispers
secrets of
darkness
lit up by
promise,
your face lit in
shadows
like the face
no one
can see.

III.
Damp breath
of evening
whispers your name.
Dew falls
all around me
hair sheltered
in mist of
sky
and blessed
rain.

IV.
Night.
Moonlight
pale on water
shows color
of your eyes,
pale shadows
of regret.

Words

I.
In young daylight
dreams of a better life
seemed possible, eventful,
within reach.
We shed our skins,
stories of a disposed
people,
remained motionless
under dawning
forecast of rest
of our lives.
In our distress,
we remembered
how the taste of joy
once interred in our hearts slowly faded
as the daylight
moved on.

II.
In my bones
I carry a story
of blessing,
of death,
of breasts cut from bodies
of dispossessed limbs,
severed from solid
trunk of speech, of
matter, of blood
and birth;
skin shorn in flakes.
It was the beginning
of the descent of stars
into my bones.

III.
Someone said once
in a famous movie,
"It's as if a thousand screaming

voices were suddenly silenced."
Silence resists.
It exits bones,
seeps through the flesh
until the sound of the lash
comes on a dappled gray ash,
settling within blood.

There is no resistance
in this ancestral form of grieving.
It takes many forms,
many refugees in the silence
of harbored secrets,
held close to where
no one can see them.
Blood and bone
is no safe place
for the missing, the murdered,
recorded generation
upon generation
until silence,
reed thin, emaciated,
takes on sallow glow
of diseased and broken
flesh.

IV.
When even walking becomes
a danger, foot in front of foot,
thinking "I must walk upright,
upright…"
Worn bits of carpet,
faded wood, and marks
upon the wall of a home
that never wanted us,
wanted us.
Words are our only weapons,
as grief grows,
swallowing knot
of feathers, bones,
and the undigested bits,

turning our steps
into shards of glass.
Bone fragments.

We are glass, ever
shattering,
at any moment.

V.
The young daylight
found me, blood drying
in early morning as
I gazed out over the burning
taste of last drop
of fire upon my tongue.
I carry voices
on my tongue,
a world where
there can be no mercy, no joy,
no thought of ever catching
the last train home.
I can't hold on,
I can't let go,
I can't put one foot in
front of another,
can't find the space of reason
to put a sentence together.
What good am I,
flying blind in this world
where words are what matters,
when the connection
between bone, blood, brain
is severed by the very
rising
of the sun in a place
where I'm not even
supposed to be?

Shedding your skin,
I step out of your shadow,
one eye to the stars,

the other,
watching the heat
of your breath
as you pull
further and further
away.

Nocturne

Voices play
In paradise pushing
edge of light
into view.
I sing with them,
My voice silent,
My mind a cacophony

My voice
sailing up
stone path
once brought
tears
of joy
to heart.

Now
same song
brings tears
of a different
kind.

The Daughter of the Sun

Washing clean
the stains of burden
and dumb luck,
she falls across
a barren world
that has yet to
remember.

Stealing
aboard a flight of protruded
dreams, she
awaits, lingers,
singing a song
that calls
to the damage of stars
and crying a deed
left unfinished.

The early morning,
light finds itself
surrounded by
in-betweens
her song varies
in length, in tone,
in vision
and breadth.

Dawn remains
A new day
when daylight
can turn either way:
towards light, towards dark.
Like her heart.
Forgiveness,
or famine,
sometimes these things,
can never remain
in the same flame,

as a heart broken
by grief and constant tongue-loosening
pride. Will she sing
as a star rises,
giving light to a world
framed in darkness?
Or, will she remain still,
looking in shadow
for pieces
of the shattered and shaking
rain crossed and shimmering
in a blessing of dawn.

III. Baskets Filled with Burdens

> Shilombish Holitopa ma!
> Ish minti pulla cha,
> Hattak ilbvsha pia ha
> Ish pi yukpalachke
>
> —Uba Isht Taloa
> (Choctaw Hymn #48)

The Other Daughter of the Sun

i.
A thin line stretches
Along an axis dotted
With starlight.
Bending back upon
Itself, grazing
At the beginning
Of the World.
Passing the reed
Through her teeth
And softening the
Crisscross grass
Four times over,
Four times back,
Weaving a pattern
Through memory, she
Chases the end of beauty
Where this story
Begins again.
Sunset,
Mother calling,
This is the advent
Of this world,
Traced along the edge
Of a non-descript star.
They are born here,
And die in their
Infancy then, a bright
Collapse in upon
Itself.
We are not unlike
the sky above us,
Stretching our arms
Up to where
We emerged.
This is no different.
The story told
In a different tongue

Will capture this loss
On film.

ii.
Ashes carry
the genes of
the thousand
lights of star,
tiny holes in
the forever sky,
The ghost of
The child left
That night she
Emerged, gasping
And someone else
Entered
In her place.
The blood memory
Of a people,
Bearing the weight
Of a map
Crossed under the
dappled starlight
upon hearts
of those who came before.
She is no different,
Her eyes open
as she crossed the bones,
muscle and slough
of her mother's
womb,
canal, entrance into this world.
Singing a song in
a language
she who birthed
will never know.

iii.
Redbird was not her only child.
Case in point:

the story passed into memory.
in memory, birthed
in blood,
in bone fragments
shattered amongst
the rocks of a stolen
tongue,
her story becomes not
her own.
Tying her down
with the lash
of their lies,
her grief bled
into skin,
Redbird
a cry away from life,
Kwi, kwi…
Fly, Redbird,
and what is left,
but a pile of bones
ground to ash
and dust
where
death resides.

Afterglow

Sunset.
This is how
we make peace.
The world centered
upon perfect
calm of entering
the next realm
of thought, of
memory.

Light is perfect.
After a glaring sun,
light is gentle here,
keeping time as it
rushes forward to
end the day.

In muted tones
we end our day.
Quiet, someone may hear.
But isn't that what we
want, here in this world
where love is a gentle
breath of wind
falling from mouths
lush from rain…?

This is how we
make love:

bodies splitting
the firmament
passing through
lips, eyes, pads of fingers,
souls. The color
of our passion is
the color of the sky
at sunset,
congealed, heavy reds,

bleeding pinks and spotting to
sharp blues fading,
to the coldness
of silver.

This is not how we
make war.

I Must Keep Myself
for Stu

I must keep myself
from dropping down
dance of a red
dawn upon a mountain
of rain,
a blessing of mist
to desert of desire.

I must keep myself
from falling off the barren
road of my Ancestors, tracing step
by step, an even
pace that takes me
farther from the road
set upon by necessity.

I must keep myself
from entering bliss
of another's desire
to retain the overseer's
mentality separating
land from blood, memory
from body, story from song
and in this force of
breath from bones
long forsaken and driven
by the light of a 1000
year old flash of starlight
and grace from a blessing
of myth,
burden of survival
in this red sunset of memory,
of time, of descendancy,

I must keep myself
from whirling in
a spiral of continuance.
Before story

can uncurl in a flame
of telling and years
of breath upon a dark
and dry wind,
it must speak
in a confluence
of ash, an arc of light,
a memory of stone
and a flash of
blood
in a memory of when
we unfurled
in a center that
was home.

The Rapture

I imagine
his hands
upon mine.
Drops of blood
form shapes
stars
moons
sun
tracing wounds
carved into
muscle
bone
his palm,
I bring my fingers
to lips
blood lacing
between my teeth,

I am saved.

Chaconne
for Maria Barbara Bach

Sadness is immeasurable
by which
your name has been
lost upon keystrokes,
upon variations
and lamentation of time
I find the imprint of your
fingers, your perfume,
your lips
painted red as tears
upon dawn.
I cannot find words
I cannot name sorrow
passing of light
passing of shadow into darkness
in your love
I find refugee, a
pauper, a prince
and I will sing no more
for voice will give
way to movement
and fingers
of bone worn to blood
I will sing a dirge
as the cortege passes.

Your lips upon mine
and my hands will follow
them, lines of variation,
lines of fading ink as it
burns red into the page.
my love, how your body
is like parchment:
the color of your skin
imbedded in thickness
and light
and darkness of a folio
of notes worn in winter.

your lips press upon
my neck, cool from the grave
and the cold earth falls from underneath
your fingers
ravaged by death
time
in fevered caresses press
upon me until song
comes bursting forth
and I burn for you
upon the empty page
writing movements
and chaconne
upon cold skin
of your stone

my love will you ever return
only in shadowed darkness
and flesh pressing upon
my hands
lips red
with the stain
of death?

Inheriting Her Brother's Horse

Walking
away from
place, stolen
like kisses
between classes,
the world shatters
upon a blood axis
and betrayal.
Keeping count
of vengeance
painted by numbers
upon our hearts,
the order is
precise.
Ones are red,
twos are black,
threes are white,
and everything else
pales in shadow,
fading to grey.
Who will keep time
in ballads of lost dreams
and hopes pinned
to the chest
of the boy dying
from a hole
in his heart?

The road looms
ahead, swimming
a mirror
reflecting sky.
She places her
hands upon worn white leather,
cracks under her fingers
lovingly filled
With layers of
every contrivance
known to boy-kind.

The crack of his skull
meets the blood
pouring from
his heart
she is amazed
she could wipe
away all of his blood
from the well-worn
white leather
interiors.
Fixing her stare
upon the mirror ahead,
not looking back, not
even once,
she pushes on,
leaving his ghost

Kama'aina
(child of the land)

"Is this world
the real one,"
she asked,
"or is the world
in my dreams – the
world that
keeps me clear
of the thread
connecting me
to what remains
inside."

"This world is
what you wish
it," I say,
She gazes
at black set eye
out to the stars
and moon
in motion
across an ocean
of memory.

Twilight

Sun falls behind
succulence of cloud.
Our coming, our leaving
another day, another night.

Water sprays
from crest
of a fluorite wave.
The head tips slightly
forward,
leading torrent
of motion
one after the other,
capping to shore.
Breaking, as grief
pushes on ahead.

Last light
shallows in her absence.
Turning, twisting,
now just an imprint
where my feet touched earth.
Trading breath,
leaves flutter
in waning daylight,
seared by rising
breath of heaven.

Like so many before,
so many after,
sho will be here
to sing
when I
am gone?

Cardinal Direction

I.
Upon a roof
made of grass, spit
and shine
and a wind from a fractal sky,
the form and shape
follows the
path of the directions
where story passes
between women.

In this foreign
land, the love of
place carries
the love of space.
The difference is
we love
for what we know
we are.

II.
Four times
we have crossed
between Redbird's world
and her mother's.
Life and
living in between —
world between souls,
and that which
ceases to fear the
light of a star
shadowed only
in
Herself.

Each time
the words are
the same.

Lovers caught
between fragmented
sentences
and eyes of
gold hearted
mourning—
We stand
and face away
not wishing to
be seen,
be heard.

Redbird, rush away
from the touch
of perfect
Warrior,
And one blemished
by stain
Of rage,
Driving the world
Away with
Fingers
forced to heal.
Compelled to carry
you home.
What will
you choose?

It's not that simple.
The story never is.

III.
Caught between every
Daughter who leaves
a Red Sun mother
To exist on
The plane
Of anger,
Of the first
Pang of knowing
He would kill.

She was a happy
Daughter of the sun
Until some man
Got cocky—as men do.
They can't help it.
Too much of a good thing.
And the sun
She was too much of a good thing,

Redbird
We are not the first daughters
Caught between
a mother
and a man.

IV.
Four times,
we have crossed
directions—
each time
fire moving
from footsteps
of woman,
singing to the sun.

Redbird loves
for she knows
no other way

than to mirror the sound
of love burning
four times
In 4/4 time
to each world
left behind.

IV. The Knot at the End of the World

Crucial to finding the way is this: there is no beginning or end. You must make your own map.

~Joy Harjo

The Water Monster

Running,
the earth
beneath me
rises
to each step
framing
halo
around
my heart.

Cool,
afternoon air
breathes gently
across my face.
Wistful, I look
to grey sky,
wishing for rain
but the ocean
breathes in
taking rain
into her mouth.

I Met an Old Woman

I met an old woman
who looked beyond
the years of living,
scattered among stones,
grain—
living between
ashes, reeds,
forgotten things.
Taking my hand
in hers.
Bébé, bébé,
she whispers—
then I am standing under
a splash of sky
spreading from center
of the womb
of hidden and swollen
stars.

In her touch,
she placed
memory rooted
and routed along
a trail of tears,
from which
spring roses
born of thorns
and deep red bloom.
Survival is this,
she said.
Biology speaking language
unspoken by stars
whose light
has long gone
back to the exploding
dome of sky.

Entrails

of luminescence, seeping into new wet
beings like a blessing.

We can trace the trajectory
of a spark, of birth
of life, of death.
Here it ends
when it begins.

Bébé, she smiles,
you look so like my own.
A motherless child
sees oceans of stars
in her eyes,
laced within
the shining sorrow
of a long foreshadowed
unfolding prayer.

Hanalei

What is the color
of moon drenched water
2000 miles from the
black light of home?

Sparse in its
brilliance,
silver, not shades
of an opposite
of shadow,
but in light.
True colors
shed their skin
bold, pure radiance
and growing
toward a sun
of brilliant gold.

Yet now
purchased from
light
shining on
opposite ends
of the world
upon a landscape
filled in sharp relief.

The Knot at the End of the World
for my aunt, Dorothy Frances Gilmore, who took her sister's place

Each knot of a curse
formed long before
The Maker of Breath sang us into life
from a cloud formed in
the crevices of the Milky Way,
this world repeats
the presence of spirits
and the land that
speaks to the past.
Can we connect
passing dots,
constellation by
constellation,
forming patterns
that the first woman
who fell through it
named into being?
Crossing water
I hear her voice
and I think I must
tear a song
from static that lives
on the air
at night. She
is no longer there.
This I have forgotten
For the thousandth time
this morning.
So many dreams.
So many graces
I have let slip and
woven into the skylight covering
my head. Entering
into the song, I
raise my hands
to the stars I
have named in her
honor. The same

star she watched
as I sang the oldest story
I knew, the
light leaving when
she was still here
with me
watching the night
sky.

Global Positioning System

Is this the realm
of the world from
the mouth
of the meridian
of hope?
Watching
black belt of
lit stars
shining home,
we look to the map
remaindered by ancestors
in times of loss,
of love, of ceremony,
of labor, of vision
and even breath
of pinpointed
tiny oceans
of star. Visible
now, they carry
the light and longing
of thousands of years,
sending a message
from the old ones
seen now
by we who remain, gazing,
through their eyes.

What moves is memory.
a map to the places they
called home pulses through
our bones, our
marrow. Blood carried upon
road to remembrance
and light.

With memory old eyes I record these
spaces of wind, of
movement,
for generations,
the constellation
cartography a memory
of what moves,
the air
that breathes.

Epilogue

o gi ye lv ha a ni
tsi do tsi la wi tsi ga
u yo s dv no ga dv nv
no ho de tsv ya ga ni
v tle s di a se quo quo
yi di tsv la we tse s di

—Abide with Me (Cherokee Hymn #2)

How we end(ed)

Kisses crafted
from parchment,
a love story
ends tragically:

Renewed,
he emerges,
steam rising
in a moonlit flare.
Rising to greet him,
Tongues tangled
between
recycled lines,
threadbare cotton
and flesh.

Watching from afar,
she places her mark upon
the cracked, pale linen —
a death song
that will toll,
rendering the march
that led them
to battle.

How much time
has passed
since she sang
her song —
for love, for luck,
for memory,
forever?

Later she gazes
at fruits from her womb,
she wonders how
different
the page would be
had the charm
meant forever.

Carolyn M. Dunn, PhD., is a Louisiana Creole whose indigenous ancestry includes Cherokee, Muskogee Creek, and Seminole descent on her father's side, and Tunica-Choctaw-Biloxi on her mother's. Born in California as a second-generation urban mestiza, her ancestral roots run deep in Louisiana, Mississippi, and Oklahoma. Her work has been recognized by the Wordcraft Circle of Storytellers and Writers as Book of the Year for poetry (*Outfoxing Coyote*, 2002) as well as the Year's Best in 1999 for her short story "Salmon Creek Road Kill," and the Native American Music Awards, for the all-woman drum group The Mankillers' CD *Comin to Getcha*.

In addition to *Outfoxing Coyote*, her books include *Through the Eye of the Deer* (Aunt Lute Books, 1999), *Hozho: Walking in Beauty* (McGraw Hill, 2002), *Coyote Speaks* (H.N. Abrams, 2008), *Echolocation: Poems, Stories and Songs from Indian Country—L.A.* (Fezziweg Press, 2013), and *The Stains of Burden and Dumb Luck*. Her plays *The Frybread Queen* and *Ghost Dance* have been developed and staged at Native Voices at the Autry in Los Angeles, and are published in the Alexander Street Press collection *New Native North American Indian Drama*. She lives in Oklahoma with her family.

www.ingramcontent.com/pod-product-compliance
Lightning Source LLC
Chambersburg PA
CBHW020958090426
42736CB00010B/1373